TRY NOT TO LAUGH CHALLENGE

AF270920

SPOOKY JOKES FOR KIDS

HUNDREDS OF SPOOKTACULAR JOKES, GHASTLY RIDDLES,
FANG-TASTIC PUNS, SILLY KNOCK-KNOCKS, TRICKY TONGUE TWISTERS
FOR HALLOWEEN & YEAR ROUND SCARY FAMILY FUN!

Howling Moon Books

© 2018 Howling Moon Books

© 2018 Illustrations by C.S. Adams

ALSO AVAILABLE BY HOWLING MOON BOOKS

SPOOKY JOKES FOR KIDS

IF YOU'RE LAUGHING, YOU'RE LOSING!

(BUT, YOU'RE HAVING LOTS OF FUN!)

Try Not to Laugh Challenge!

Rules:

Pick your team, or go one on one.

Sit across from each other & make eye contact.

Take turns reading jokes to each other.

You can make silly faces, funny sound effects, etc.

When your opponent laughs, you get a point!

First team to win 3 points, **Wins!**

If you're laughing, you're losing!
(But you are having lots of fun!)

How do jack-o-lanterns cross
the road?

The cross gourd!

What happens when jack-o-lanterns
don't listen to the cross gourds?

Squash!

How do witches stay in shape?

They hex-ercise!

Why did the little ghost go to the doctor?

To get his BOO-ster shot!

What spell did the little witch use before her test?

Hocus Focus!

Why don't mummies have friends?

They are too wrapped up in themselves!

What is a witch's favorite song?

Ghouls just want to have fun!

What kind of care package do you send a witch at summer camp?

A scare package!

What did the skeleton order at
the restaurant?

Spare ribs!

What kind of pants do ghosts wear?

BOO jeans!

What kind of sandwich do
ogres eat?

Gross beef sandwich!

What did the ghoul buy for his house?

A flat scream TV!

What did the ghoul's flat scream TV come with?

A one-year Scare-antee!

What does the Abominable Snowman eat?

Ice burgers!

Why wasn't the unicorn witch scary?

Because she was too uni-corny!

What did the unicorn witch say
when she fell off of her broom?

I've fallen and I can't giddy-up

How does Dracula feel when the night
is over?

Dead on his feet!

How do you say goodbye to a vampire?

So long sucker!

What do ghosts do with bubble gum?

They blow BOO-bles!

What are a monster's favorite days
of the week?

Moan-days and Fright-days!

What do vampires do when they
get sleepy?

They take a coffin break!

Why wasn't Frankenstein happy about
his 500 social media followers?

They all had torches and pitchforks!

What mythical creature is a slob?

The Lock Mess Monster!

Who lives in the scary hundred acre wood?

Winnie the BOO!

How are witch books held together?

They are spellbound!

How do witches use math to break a curse?

They use a hex-a-gone!

Why do skeletons dislike snow?

Because it chills them to the bone!

What computer search engine does a gargoyle use?

He goo-goyles!

Why doesn't the ghoul like to give out his cell phone number?

He likes to scream his calls!

What musical instrument does the invisible ghoul play?

Air guitar!

What famous painter does the
giant blob like?

Vincent Van Goo!

What do you call someone who is
afraid of Halloween?

A Hallo-weenie!

Who is the most powerful potato
in the galaxy?

Darth Tater!

What monster is the best dancer?

The boogie man!

What ancient building do monsters
visit in Rome?

The Colo-scream-um!
(Colosseum)

What fountain do ghosts visit in
Rome?

Trev-eeee Fountain!
(Trevi Fountain)

What is the swamp creature's
favorite dessert?

Key Slime Pie!

How do you get a skeleton in a
good mood?

You tickle his funny bone!

What kind of car does Dracula drive?

The Bat-mobile!

What song do vampires never
listen to?

Sunshine on my shoulders make
me happy!

Why are vampires good at getting
ships through bad storms?

Because they know how to bat-ten
down the hatches!

What did the pirate say when
it spotted the ghost whale?

Thar she BOOS!

Why did the invisible boy have
trouble in math class?

He couldn't use his fingers to count!

Why doesn't the invisible ghoul get
invitations to Halloween parties?

Because you know he will never
show up!

 Knock, knock.
Who's there?
Freddie.
Freddie who?

Freddie or not, here comes
Halloween!

Knock, knock.
Who's there?
Irish.
Irish who?

Irish you a Happy Halloween!

Knock, knock.
Who's there?
Howl.
Howl who?

Howl will we scare Mom!

Knock, knock.
Who's there?
Weirdo.
Weirdo who?

Weirdo we go to scare more
people!

What is a troll's favorite food?

You!

Who makes frog monsters?

Dr. Frogenstein!

What did the astronaut cook in
his skillet?

Unidentified frying objects!
(UFOs)

What did the vampire doctor yell
out in his waiting room?

Necks, please!

Why did the invisible ghoul put on
his sunglasses?

So he could take a selfie!

Why are skeletons so calm?

Because nothing gets under
their skin!

Why did the headless horseman go
into business for himself?

He wanted to get a head in life!

What do ghouls drink on a hot day?

Ice-ghoul lemonade!

What search engine do ghosts like?

BOO-gle!

What is Dracula's favorite dog?

A bloodhound!

Did you hear about the mummy who wished he could fly a broomstick.

It was witch-ful thinking!

What is the werewolf's favorite day?

Moon-day!

What turns off the lights on Halloween?

A light witch!

Why are teachers happy on Halloween?

Because there is a lot of school spirit!

What can you say about
the bad mummy joke?

It Sphinx!

What is a classic slime movie?

Goo with the Wind!

What did the pirate say when it snowed on Halloween?

Shiver me timbers!

Where do pirates like to keep their Halloween candy?

In their treasu-arrrrrr chest!

What were baby slime's first words?

Goo-goo!

Who is tall, green, and slimy?

Franken-Slime!

Why did the little witch bring a
bale of hay to bed every night?

To feed her nightmares!

What blog do monsters like to read
every day?

A horror-scope blog!

What kind of bath do little ghosts like?

BOO-ble baths!

What is a ghost's favorite train to ride in?

The caBOO-se!

Who were the first monsters to fly?

The Fright Brothers!

Why is Dracula finishing a big meal
like 3 balls and 2 strikes?

They are both full counts!

What do ghouls like to ride at the amusement park?

The scary-go-round!

What do you call a ghoul with a broom?

The grim sweeper!

What is a monster's favorite cheese?

Munster-ella!

Why did the werewolf give up acting?

Because he couldn't find a part he
could sink his teeth in!

What kind of streets do zombies
live on?

Dead ends!

What do monsters eat with their sand-witch?

Ghoul-slaw!

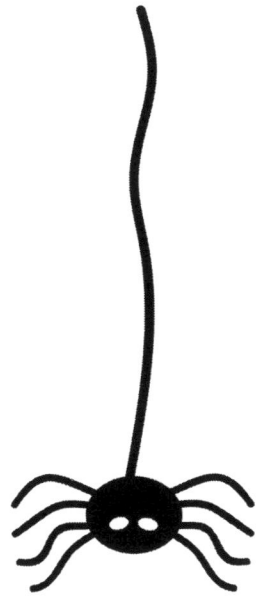

What do spiders eat in Paris?

French flies!

What do you say when you go
inside a haunted house?

Who ghost there!

Why are scarecrows always tired?

Because they never get to hit
the hay!

Why didn't the skeleton want any
Halloween candy?

He didn't have the stomach for it!

Why did the vampire joke flop?

Because it was a vein attempt
at humor!

How do monsters get ready
for college?

Graduate from High Ghoul!

What part of a ship does an ogre
like the best?

The poop deck!

What is a werewolf's favorite book?

Hairy Potter!

How does Hairy Potter get rid
of his rash?

Quit-itch!

Knock, knock.
Who's there.
Les.
Les who?

Les go Trick or Treating!

Knock, knock.
Who's there?
Philip.
Philip who?

Philip my bag with candy!

Knock, knock.
Who's there?
Maia.
Maia who?

Maia Halloween candy is all gone!

Knock, knock.
Who's there?
Ken.
Ken who?

Ken we get some more candy?

What does a panda ghost eat?

Bam-BOO!

Where do ghouls go on vacation?

BOO-hamas!

What did the teacher say to the mummies at the end of the school day?

Time to wrap things up!

Why couldn't the little ghost see his parents?

They were transparents!

Where do ogres go to college?

P. U. University!

What kind of phone does an ogre have?

A smellular phone!

What kind of camp do flying broomsticks go to?

Sweep-away camp!

How did the witch give directions to the haunted house?

Fright this way!

Tongue Twisters

Wicked wrappers.

Goey goon glitter.

Swell spell.

Which witch wants wet warts.

Scary screechy scream.

What do you get when you cross
a vampire and a duck?

Count Quackula!

What does a vampire say when you
give him Halloween candy?

Fangs a lot!

What is the swamp monster's
favorite game?

Slimon Says!

What did the frog wear on
Halloween?

A prince costume!

What do southern ghosts say?

BOO Y'all!

Why did the giant bee join the rock band?

He wanted to be the lead stinger!

Why did the ghoul put boo-berries in his guitar?

He wanted to have a jam session!

What monster is always buying new clothes?

A werewolf!

What is a monster's favorite food?

Ghoul-ash!

What is the safest room to be in if a ghost is in your house?

The living room!

Why did the skeleton cat jump on the cruise ship?

She heard it was a bone voyage!

What do you call a scary sheep herder?

Little BOO Peep!

Who is scary and lives in a pineapple under the sea?

Sponge Blob Scare Pants!

Why did the monster hang a "Go Away" sign on his door?

It was his terror-tory!

Where do zombies go golfing?

At the golf corpse!

What do you call a ghost that is
good at magic tricks?

BOO-dini!

What is an ogre's favorite dessert?

Eyes cream!

Why is it so easy to fool vampires?

Because they are suckers!

What is a monster's favorite painting?

Moan-a-Lisa!

What do call a cold ghost?

Casp-brrr!

What do monsters drink on Halloween
to stay awake?

Coffin-ated Coffee!

What is a ghost's favorite fairy tale?

Sleeping BOO-ty!

Why shouldn't you give Big Foot
baked beans?

It would be a gas-tly mistake!

How do you know if Big Foot has been
in your pumpkin patch?

You will be left with Squash!

What is a ogre's favorite pastry?

Ick-clairs!

What does a monster study in college?

Ick-onomics!

How do monsters greet each other
in the morning?

Happy moaning!

How do Irish monsters greet each
other in the morning?

Top of the moaning!

What do vampires brush their
teeth with?

Fang-paste!

What do monsters do after they
brush their fangs?

They gargoyle with mouthwash!

What do you call the next day
in a graveyard?

Tomb-orrow!

Why was the ghost's message
so scary?

Because it was an eeeeeee-mail!

What kind of dinner do little monsters like?

Spook-ghetti!

What skeleton is really good at solving mysteries?

Sherlock Bones!

What is a ghoul's favorite song?

Shrieking in the Rain!

What is the scariest bug in
the world?

A zom-bee!

What kind of dinosaurs casts spells?

Tyrannosaurus hex!

What does a witch's motorcycle
sound like?

Broooom Broooom!

Why didn't the ghost buy
a new Halloween costume?

Because the price was out of sight!

Why don't witches go on cruise ships?

They get potion sickness!

What kind of dances do witches go to?

Crystal Balls!

What is black and white and dead all over?

A vampire cow!

What do you do if your GPS stops working?

Ask a where-wolf!

Why do vampires like baseball?

They like to play with all the bats!

Who is coming to your house on
Halloween if you give out cookies?

The Cookie Monster!

Where does the giant blob live
in London?

Muckingham Palace!

Why couldn't the werewolf and
sheep be friends?

Because they had mutton in
common!

Why didn't the baby sea monster
bite the fish hook?

He wasn't ready for the reel world!

On what day do Trolls eat people?

Chewsday!

What do you call an ogre's robot?

R2PU!

What is an ogre's favorite song?

Somewhere Ogre the Rainbow!

What happened when the bat flew
into the wind mill?

Shredded eek!

What do ghosts like to eat for
breakfast?

BOO-berry pancakes!

What do you get when you cross a
vampire with soda?

Count Dra-cola!

What is a ghost full of when it
has a cold?

BOO-gers!

What is a wizard's favorite song?

I Wand-a Hold your Hand!

Why shouldn't you tell Dracula
your problems?

Because he will give you bat advice!

Why is it safe to tell your secret
to a mummy?

Because they keep everything
under wraps!

How do you fix a broken
jack-o-lantern?

With a pumpkin patch!

What did the jack-o-lantern say
to the pumpkin?

Cut it out!

What kind of truck does
Frankenstein drive?

A monster truck!

Where does Frankenstien like to
go fishing?

Lake Eerie!

Knock, knock.
Who's there?
Justin.
Justin who?

Justin time for Halloween!

Knock, knock.
Who's there?
Olive.
Olive who?

Olive Halloween!

Knock, knock.
Who's there?
Lenny.
Lenny who?

Lenny in, there's a monster chasing me!

Knock, knock.
Who's there?
Diane.
Diane who?

I am Diane out here, let me in!

How does a cornfield look on Halloween?

Very EAR-ie!

How do you keep flys out of a monster's house?

A scream door!

Why did Dracula return his computer?

Because he wanted it to have
more bytes!

How do you make a sundae for
a ghost?

With ice scream and BOO-nanas!

What kind of marathons do
vampires like to sign up for?

Bite-athons!

What do you call a cat that likes
to drink blood?

A vampurr!

Where do ghosts go to get their
hair done?

The BOO-ty parlor!

How did all the vampires know the
Halloween party was cancelled?

Bat news travels fast!

Why did the policeman give a
ticket to the ghost?

He didn't have a haunting license!

Why did the Cyclops close his school down?

He only had one pupil!

Why did the little vampire wear a hat to school?

Because she was having a bat hair day!

What is a vampire's favorite movie?

The Bat News Bears!

Where do ghosts post their pictures?

On Face-BOO-k!

Why was the alphabet sad?

They heard about the Dead C!
(Dead Sea)

Why was the little vampire in
time out?

Because she had a bat attitude!

What do you call a magical ghost?

Ghosticorn!

Why was the ghoul always broke?

Because a ghoul and his money
are soon parted!

What did the three-headed dog say
to the skeleton?

We have bones to pick with you!

What is it like to ride a dragon?

It is terror-flying!

What trees do ghosts like the best?

Ceme-trees!

What was the name of the skeleton
rock band?

The Rolling Bones!

What kind of tea do witches make?

Nas-tea!

What do ghouls wear on Halloween?

Cos-tombs!

Why do zombies like to stay at
the graveyard hotel?

They have tomb service!

What kind of engagement ring do
you give an ogre?

A stye-mond ring!

Where do werewolves stay on vacation?

Howl-iday Inn!

What is a ghoul's favorite breakfast?

Scream of Wheat!

What do you call a scary droid?

BOO 2D2!

What is a ghost's favorite book?

Black BOO-ty!

What do you get when you give
a witch's cat a lemon?

A scary sour puss!

What monsters sell the most cookies?

The Ghoul Scouts!

Why shouldn't you make a big dinner
for a vampire?

Because they eat necks to nothing!

Is Frankenstein a fast eater?

Yup, he bolts his food down!

So, what monster eats the fastest?

A goblin!

How did we know the ghost
was innocent?

He had an ali-BOO!

What do ghosts bring to the beach?

BOO-kinis and sun scream!

Why did the witch fail her
potions class?

She forgot to use spell check!

What do monsters eat for dessert?

Boston scream pie!

What should everyone be afraid of?

Monster BOO-gers!

How did the ghost give directions
to the cemetery?

The graveyard is dead ahead!

What do you call a slimy goblin?

A goo-blin!

What does a witch do when her magic potion doesn't work?

Call hex support!

Why was the witch excited to go to college?

Because she was going to meet her broom mate!

Who is a pumpkin most afraid of?

Cinderella's fairy godmother!

How did Cinderella get to the
Halloween ball?

Her scary godmother!

What do you call an ogre who can predict the future?

A fortune smeller!

Why was the ogre's nose sad?

Because it didn't get picked!

Where do little vampires go
in September?

Bat to school!

What is a baby vampire's favorite
game?

Batty-cake!

What happens in the graveyard bathroom?

Creep-pee!

Why are baby monsters so cute?

Because they are not fully groan!

How do monsters like their eggs?

Terri-fried!

Why do monsters like marathons?

Because they like fast food!

What does Big Foot say on Halloween?

Trick or Feet!

What is Sasquach's favorite game?

Hide and seek!

Spooky Rhyme Time!

What do you call ghost slime?

BOO goo!

What do you call a bunch of vampires?

A fang gang!

What do you call a mummy who
eats cookies in bed?

A crummy mummy!

What do you call a snail's cry?

A snail wail!

What do you call an amphibian that
has magical powers?

A wizard lizard!

What do you call a monster cheer?

A fear cheer!

What do you call a special ghost party?

A ghost roast!

What is worse than a giant blob?

A blob mob!

What is another name for Halloween?

Fright night!

What do you call a witch's favorite potion?

A swell spell!

What do you call a witch with magic powers that don't always work?

A witch glitch!

What happened to the bat that flew
into the tree?

A bat splat!

What do you call an Abominable
Snowman who is inconsiderate?

A petty Yeti!

What happens when something
slimes all your Halloween candy?

A slime crime!

What do you call an ogre who makes people laugh?

A joker ogre!

What does a naughty troll get for Christmas?

Troll coal!

Where do Native American ghosts live?

Creepy teepees!

What do you call an adult monster
in school?

A creature teacher!

What do you call a friendly mummy?

A chummy mummy!

What do you call a weird ghost?

A shriek freak!

What do you call a monster after he eats?

A wobblin' goblin!

What do you call a spoiled bat?

A bat brat!

What do you call a witch who drinks too much coffee?

A twitchy witchy!

What do you call a ghost house cleaner?

A neat sheet!

Where do vampires live?

Vampsterdam!

Where do vampires buy their school supplies?

Pencil-vein-ia!

Why didn't the ogre laugh at the joke?

Because it went ogre his head!

What is an ogre's favorite Christmas movie?

Grandma Got Run Ogre by a Reindeer!

Why do ghosts go to college?

To get a dead-ucation!

What does a skeleton say
before he eats?

Bone appetit!

What was the monster's favorite
class in school?

Home ick-onomics!

Why are zombies good artists?

Because they draw lots of flies!

Tongue Twisters

Messy moldy mummy makeup.

Ghosts grasping garlic gourds.

Zany zombie zebra zoo.

Freddie the Yeti is ready.

Tickle T. Rex ticklish toes.

What do the military say on Halloween?

BOO-yah!

What do retired ghosts say?

Those were the Ghoul old days!

When do monsters like to play silly pranks on each other?

April Ghoul's Day!

What is a monster's favorite painter?

Moan-et! (Monet)

What do mummies wait for all year?

Mummy's Day!

Knock, knock.
Who's there?
Bea.
Bea who?

Bea-ware, Halloween is coming!

Knock, knock.
How's there?
Howl.
Howl who?

Howl come we are going in the
haunted house?

Knock, knock.
Who's there?
Manuel.
Manuel who?

Manuel be sorry if you
go into that haunted house!

Knock, knock.
Who's there?
Wool.
Wool who?

Wool you scream if you see
anything scary?

Knock, knock.
Who's there?
Jacklyn.
Jacklyn who?

Jacklyn Hyde!

Knock, knock.
Who's there?
Voodoo.
Voodoo who?

Voodoo you think you are going
to be for Halloween?

Knock, knock.
Who's there?
Jacky.
Jacky who?

The glowing Jacky lanterns are
very scary!

Knock, knock.
Who's there?
Bat.
Bat who?

Bat you are glad those Jacky
lanterns are going out!

What is Frankenstein's favorite
ice cream flavor?

Shock-olate!

Why do dragons sleep all day?

So they can fight knights!

What is a werewolf's favorite dance?

Fang-dango!

What is a werewolf's favorite
nursery rhyme?

Hairy had a little lamb!

Why do monster children go to
bed early?

They hope to have nightmares!

Why was Dracula upset?

Because he was having a bat day!

Why did Count Dracula win an award
at the art show?

Because he was the best
at drawing blood!

Why can't zombies afford to go
out to eat?

It always costs them an arm
and a leg!

What is higher than a giant's head?

His hat!

What is brown and has lots of sticky parts?

A tree!

What room do ghouls try to stay away from?

The living room!

Why was the witch's broomstick late?

It over-swept!

What do witches wear to bed?

Fright-gowns!

Knock, knock.
Who's there?
Ivana.
Ivana who?

Ivana stay away from that
scary graveyard!

Knock, knock.
Who's there?
Window.
Window who?

Window you think we will be
far away from that graveyard!

Knock, knock.
Who's there?
Alfie.
Alfie who?

Alfie better when that vampire
is gone!

Knock, knock.
Who's there?
Handsome.
Handsome who?

Handsome garlic to me, that
vampire is coming back!

What is a ghoul's favorite play?

Romeo and Ghouliet!

What single cell organism comes
out at Halloween?

An amoe-BOO!
(amoeba)

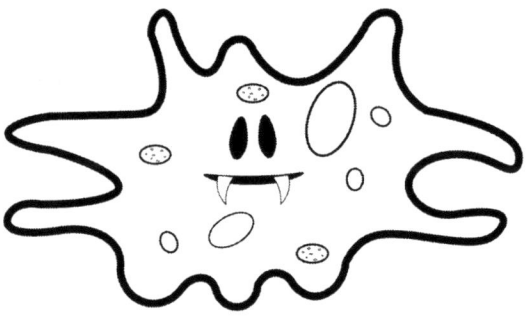

What does the monster family like to
do at amusement parks?

Ride the roller ghoster!

What did the alien vampire say when he landed on earth?

Take me to your bleeder!

What did the werewolf say when he arrived home?

Hair I am!

How do you put baby werewolves to sleep?

Growl-lbies!

What kind of music does the monster
band play?

Rock and troll!

What kind of music does the mummy
band play?

Wrap music!

What ghost ate the three bears' porridge?

Ghoul-dilocks!

What vampire loves to eat?

Count Snackula!

What do you call a jack-o-lantern's band-aid?

A pumpkin patch!

Where does Dracula Jr. like to play every night?

In the bat tub!

Why do Cyclops get along?

They see eye to eye!

What do trick or treaters eat
for Halloween?

Mask-potatoes and grave-y!

What do you get when you cross a droid and road construction?

R2-Detour!

What is the definition of extinct?

A dead skunk!

Why wouldn't you want a vampire to decorate your house?

Because they have bat taste!

What is the giant blob's favorite bird?

Swallow!

Where do ogres go to buy frog legs
& eye of newt?

The gross-ery store!

Where do ghouls get their clothes
cleaned?

The dry screamers!

What show does the monster watch
when he wants to fix up his house?

Gnome Improvement!

Why couldn't the scarecrow remember his name?

Because everything goes in one ear and out the other!

Why is the droid angry?

People keep pushing his buttons!

What do vampires like on their mashed potatoes?

Grave-y!

Who is invited to parents day at the monster school?

Mummies and Deadies!

What runs around the haunted house
but does not move?

The fence!

What needs to be fed to stay alive,
but will die if you give it water?

Fire!

Why did the werewolf student recieve an A+?

Because he was a fang-tastic student!

Where do vampires shop?

Bat-ologs!

Why are monsters famous for throwing Halloween parties?

Because they are always spook-tacular!

Why didn't the skeleton want to go to work?

Because his heart wasn't in it!

Why do monsters speak Latin?

Because it's a dead language!

What is a ghost's favorite city?

BOO York City!

Where do ghosts go hiking?

The BOO Ridge Mountains!

Why was the baby ghost crying?

Because he had a boo-boo!

Why did the witch stay in bed?

She needed to rest for a spell!

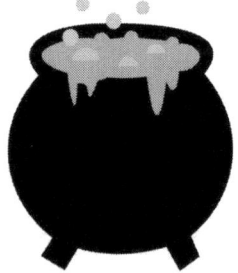

What do birds say on Halloween?

Trick or Tweet!

Where do ghosts go for lobster?

BOO-ston, Massachusetts!

What contests are witches good at?

Spell-ing bees!

What is a skeleton's favorite park?

Yellow-bone National Park!

How do aliens hold up their
space pants?

Asteroid belts!

What do you call an alien who lives
in a bog?

A marsh-in!

What is a vampire's favorite
picnic food?

Fang-furters!

Why didn't Count Dracula ever
get married?

Because he likes being a bat-chelor!

Why should you never cross a teacher with a vampire?

Because you will get lots of blood tests!

Why did the ghost join the cheer squad?

She heard they needed more school spirit!

What kind of trees do vampires
put in their garden?

Neck-tarine trees!

What does a vampire never order
at a restaurant?

Stake!

What song do ghosts sing on
July 4th?

America the BOO-tiful!

What did the witch say to the ghost?

Get a life!

What do you call a sick ghost?

An ill-usion!

What did the monster say to the invisible ghoul?

Long time no see!

How did the witch fly without her broomstick?

She witch-hiked!

What kind of veggies do ghosts like?

Tomb-atoes!

What do baby vampires take
every night?

A blood bath!

Where do famous werewolves go?

The Monster Howl of Fame!

Why was the werewolf mad?

Because a policeman gave him
a barking ticket!

Why did the giant blob eat the North Pole?

It wanted a frozen dinner!

Why was the calender so scared?

Because the calender's days were numbered!

What do wizards put on their floors?

Magic carpets!

What kind of pep talk do you
give a ghost?

An inspirational screech!

Why was the monster happy about
being picked for the Olympic team?

Because he wanted a ghoul metal!

How does Dracula find his way at night when he changes into a bat?

We don't know, he just wings it!

Who won the zombie war?

No one, it was dead even!

How much does a museum full of
skeletons weigh?

A skele-ton!

Why is it hard for a zombie to keep
a secret?

Everything he says is a
dead giveaway!

How do ghosts fix their computer problems?

They re-BOO-t them!

What kind of TV do vampires have?

Plasma TVs!

What is a baby ghost's favorite game?

Peek-a-BOO!

What do ghosts use to light their homes?

Fright bulbs!

What branch of the military did
the ogre sign up for?

The Gross Guard!

Why was it clear that the ghost
had no children?

Because he is not ap-parent!

Where do vampires vacation
in California?

San Fang-cisco!

Where do zombies want to build
a beach house?

On the Dead Sea!

Why are pumpkins so funny?

Because they are the pun-kings!

How do trees get on their computer?

They log in!

What kind of flowers do monsters grow?

Mari-ghouls!

What kind of birds like graveyards?

Ghoul-finches!

Who's the smartest ghoul in the graveyard?

Albert Frightingstein!

What do you get when you cross
a cow and a vampire?

Count Dracow-la!

What kind of school do baby
monsters go to?

Day scare centers!

What don't vampires use mouthwash?

They want bat breath!

Why isn't the Abominable Snowman
afraid of people?

Because he doesn't believe in them!

How do vampires go fishing?

In blood vessels!

How did the werewolf become the president of his company?

He clawed his way to the top!

Where do werewolves live?

The beast coast!

Where do all the famous dragons go?

Hall of Flame!

Why did the baseball players want
gnomes on their team?

They are hoping for lots of
gnome runs!

Knock, knock.
Who's there?
Atlas.
Atlas who?

Atlas it's dark outside, let's go to the haunted house!

Knock, knock.
Who's there?
Water.
Water who?

Water chances for getting out of the haunted house alive?!

Knock, knock.
Who's there?
Distinct.
Distinct who?

Distinct in this monster house
is terrible!

Knock, knock.
Who's there?
Dozen.
Dozen who?

Dozen anyone know how to get
out of this stinky house?

Knock, knock.
Who's there?
Denise.
Denise who?

My Denise are knocking in this
haunted house!

Knock, knock.
Who's there?
Ima.
Ima who?

Ima out of here!

Knock, knock.
Who's there?
Berry.
Berry who?

I'm berry excited to be a unicorn
for Halloween!

Knock, knock.
Who's there?
Latte.
Latte who?

It's latte fun scaring people
on Halloween!

Knock, knock.
Who's there?
Eye.
Eye who?

Eye think Halloween is scary!

Knock, knock.
Who's there?
Gladys.
Gladys who?

Gladys the last Halloween joke!

HOWLING MOON BOOKS

Made in the USA
Lexington, KY
26 October 2018